Contents

KU-493-709

Some words are printed in bold, **like this**. You can find out what they mean in the glossary. You can also look in the box at the bottom of the page where the word first appears.

What Is A Hero?

There are many kinds of heroes. Some heroes are famous. Other heroes are ordinary people. Animals can be heroes, too.

A hero is brave

"What's a hero? I didn't even think about it", said Uli Derickson. She worked on a plane that was **hijacked** in 1985. Everyone on board was in great danger.

Derickson **persuaded** the hijackers to let some passengers go free. The hijackers warned they would kill people unless the plane got more fuel. Derickson paid for the fuel with her own credit card!

Derickson (centre) won the Silver Cross award for valour.

hijack	take over an aeroplane using violence
persuade	talk someone into doing something
valour	bravery

HEROES WHO BRAVED SNOW AND ICE

In 1925, many children in Nome, Alaska, were sick and dying. They would die if they did not get medicine quickly. But the medicine they needed was far away. The only way to get it to Nome was by dog sled.

A race to save lives

Each dog sled team raced to meet the next one, passing on the medicine. It was like a **relay race**. In total, twenty dog sled teams travelled 1,085 kilometres (674 miles). They did this in five-and-a-half days. These human and dog heroes got the medicine to Nome. They saved hundreds of lives.

relay race	race in which each person races only part of the way, taking it in turns

The Iditarod race is held every year in Alaska to remember the heroes of 1925.

ALASKA

Nome

Nenana

Iditarod

Seward

0 50 100 Miles
0 50 100 Kilometres

---- 1925 Medicine route
—— Iditarod race route

Fascinating fact

The Iditarod dog sled race follows part of the path of the heroes.

LANCE ARMSTRONG

At the age of 25 Lance Armstrong was one of the world's best cyclists. Then, he found out he had cancer. He had two operations to treat the cancer.

A winner lives strong

After the operations, Armstrong was weak. Still, he had hope and courage. A few years later, Armstrong went on to win the Tour de France bicycle race seven times. "Before cancer, I just lived," he said. "Now I live strong."

Fascinating fact

Armstrong set up a charity. The Lance Armstrong Foundation raises money to help cancer patients.

foundation   organization that helps those in need

The Tour de France is a three-week-long bicycle race.

People wear wristbands to show they support Armstrong's charity.

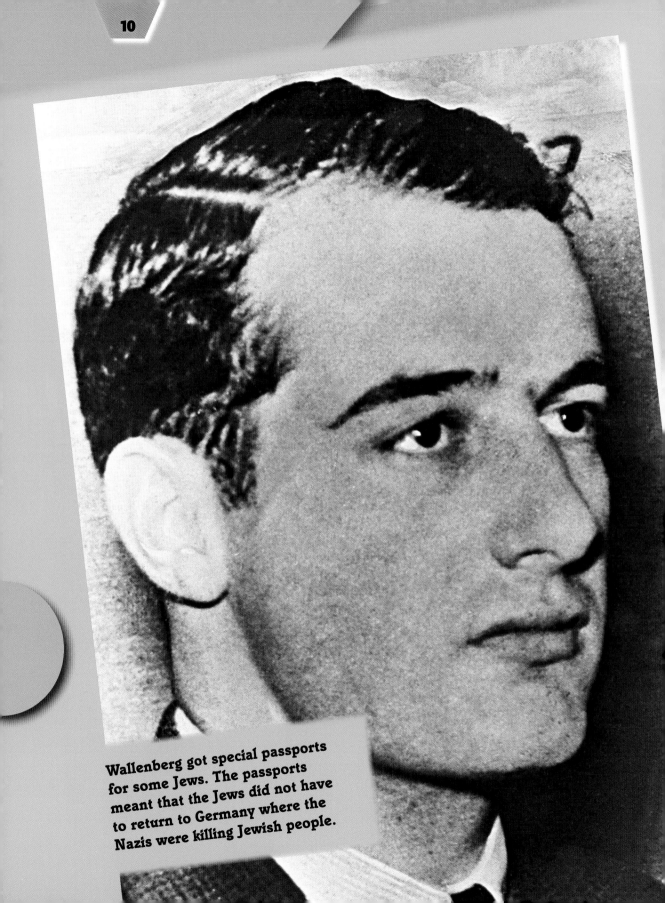

Wallenberg got special passports for some Jews. The passports meant that the Jews did not have to return to Germany where the Nazis were killing Jewish people.

HERO OF WORLD WAR II

In 1944, the **Nazis** in Germany were planning to kill 100,000 Jewish people. The Jews lived in a country called Hungary. Raoul Wallenberg found out about the plan.

Saving Jewish lives

Wallenberg helped many Jews hide. Then he told a Nazi general that killing the Jews would be a **war crime.** This scared the general. He called off the killings. In this way, Wallenberg saved more than 10,000 Jewish lives.

Fascinating fact

Wallenberg was arrested in 1945 because some people thought he was a spy. He has not been seen since.

Nazis	political party that controlled Germany from 1933 to 1945
war crime	crime committed during a war, such as killing people or treating prisoners very badly

HEROES OF SEPTEMBER 11

On September 11, 2001, a **terrorist** group called **al-Qaeda** flew planes into the World Trade Center in New York, United States. Terrorists attack and scare people. On this day, they killed thousands of people.

Just doing a job

People rushed out of the burning twin towers. As they left, firefighters ran into the buildings to help. Many people think firefighters are heroes. "We're just doing our jobs", said firefighter Kenny Haskell.

Kenny Haskell's two brothers were also firefighters. They died with many others when the twin towers collapsed.

al-Qaeda	group behind the September 11, 2001 attacks in the United States
terrorist	person who attacks and scares other people

Firefighters wanted to save lives on September 11, 2001. They had to go into dangerous areas.

Police rescue dogs searched for survivors.

Rivera (centre) said Salty's actions were "amazing".

Heroic Dogs of September 11

Omar Eduardo Rivera is blind. He was working in the World Trade Center, New York, when the planes hit.

A best friend

Rivera said, "I could hear how pieces of glass were flying around and falling. I could feel the smoke filling up my lungs."

Rivera has a **guide dog** called Salty. He set Salty free to escape the fires. However, Rivera said, "He returned to my side a few minutes later and guided me down 70 flights of stairs and out into the street."

Fascinating fact

A rescue dog helped locate a woman who was buried alive on September 11, 2001.

guide dog	dog trained to help blind people
rescue dog	dog trained to find people

People climbed onto roofs to be rescued by the helicopter team.

HEROES OF HURRICANE KATRINA

Hurricane Katrina was a deadly storm that hit the United States in August 2005. New Orleans was flooded. Many people drowned. Others climbed as high as they could and waited for help.

Helicopter rescue

There were 420 people on the roof of a hotel. Michael Sorjonen was chief of a helicopter team. His team made nearly 30 difficult helicopter trips to rescue people. It took ten hours, but the rescue mission was a success. Everyone was saved.

hurricane	powerful storm with strong winds and a lot of rain

Reeve played Superman in films, but he was a hero in real life, too.

paralysed   not able to move parts of the body

CHRISTOPHER REEVE

In 1995, "Superman" Christopher Reeve fell off a horse and broke his neck. He was **paralysed**. He could not move below his neck or breathe without help from a machine.

A hero gives hope to others

At first doctors said Reeve would never improve, but he did not give up. "The only limits you have are those you put on yourself", he said. After a while he began to breathe on his own. He got some feeling back in one finger. This meant that he could use a wheelchair.

Reeve died in 2004. Thanks to him, doctors now have hope that paralysed people can make progress.

Reeve never gave up hope.

SURFER HERO

Scott Larsen was surfing in Okinawa, Japan, when he saw a woman drowning. A strong tide had pulled her a long way from the beach.

Water rescue

First, Larsen helped her up onto his surfboard. Then he saw a man on a small raft who was also in trouble. So Larsen tied the raft to his surfboard. Then he paddled back to the beach with the woman on his surfboard and pulling the man on the raft.

CHINA

JAPAN

PACIFIC OCEAN

Okinawa

SOUTH CHINA SEA

PHILIPPINES

Fascinating fact

Larsen is American. His family moved to Japan because of his parents' jobs.

Larsen used his surfing skills and his training as a lifeguard in his daring rescue.

The **thatched** roofs of the cottages were completely destroyed.

EDDIE YOUNG

One summer night in 2005, Eddie Young was driving in Oxford. He saw flames leaping from a row of houses.

Time to be a hero

At once, Young stopped his car and ran into a burning house. He carried a 93-year-old woman out. Then he helped several other people escape the smoke and flames.

"If we were five minutes too early, we might not have seen the fire", Young said. "And if I didn't see it, these people might have all been dead."

Fascinating fact

In the UK, house fire deaths have gone down in the last few years. This is thanks to modern smoke alarms.

| thatched | roof covering of straw or reeds |

CAT HERO

In 1996, an old building in New York, United States, was on fire. A mother cat and her four-week-old kittens were caught inside.

A daring rescue

The cat was badly burned, but she did not give up on saving her kittens. A firefighter said, "She ran in and out of that building five times. She got them all out. Then she started moving the kittens one by one across the street."

Fascinating fact

The cat was called Scarlett because she had red, burned patches on her skin. Her fur soon grew back.

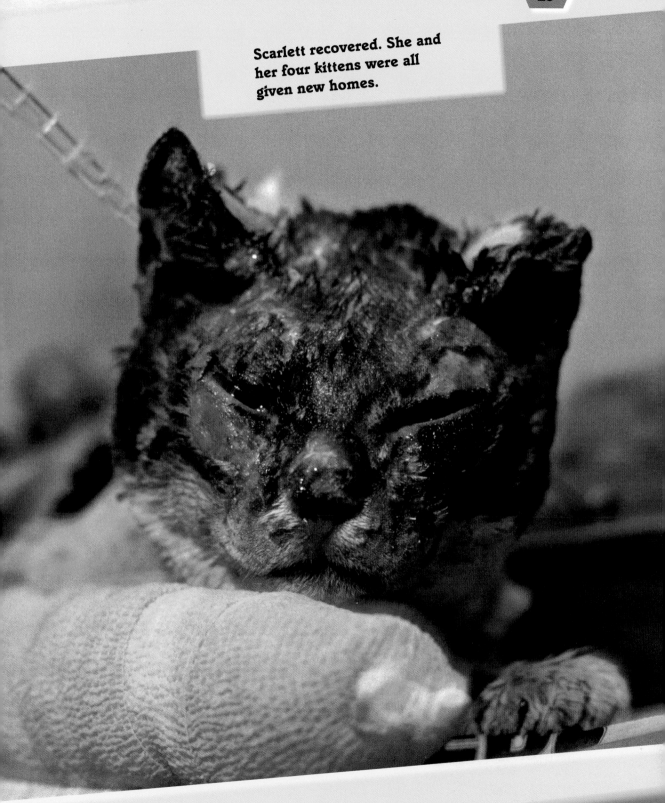

Scarlett recovered. She and her four kittens were all given new homes.

Lulu is an eastern grey kangaroo like this one.

KANGAROO HERO

In 2003, farmer Len Richards from Australia was knocked **unconscious** by a tree branch. No one knew he was hurt, except his pet kangaroo Lulu.

Lulu to the rescue

Lulu "barked like a dog", said Len's daughter Celeste. "She was obviously trying to get our attention because she never acts like that."

Thanks to Lulu, the family found Len. "If it wasn't for her, my dad could have died", Celeste said. "Lulu is my hero."

Fascinating fact

Lulu became famous. She appeared on TV programmes in Australia.

unconscious   knocked out, not awake

Great Heroes

All the heroes in this book were brave. They took risks to help others. They did not give up.

Free The Children

In 1995, twelve-year-old Craig Kielburger started an organization called Free The Children. Craig is from Toronto, Canada. He read about a boy of his age in Pakistan. The boy was killed for complaining about the way children in Pakistan were forced to work. Craig thought the boy was a hero, because he had given his life to help his friends.

Craig said, "I suddenly understood that a young person can make a difference." So he set up Free The Children to help young people around the world.

Fascinating fact

Free The Children youth volunteers raise money. They have raised enough to build 430 schools in 21 countries.

Craig spends his life helping children in many countries.

Glossary

al-Qaeda group behind the September 11, 2001, attacks in the United States

foundation organization that helps those in need

guide dog dog trained to help blind people

hijack take over an aeroplane using violence

hurricane powerful storm with strong winds and a lot of rain

Nazi political party that controlled Germany from 1933 to 1945. Adolf Hitler led this party during World War II.

paralysed not able to move parts of the body

persuade talk someone into doing something

relay race race in which each person races only part of the way, taking it in turns

rescue dog dog trained to find people

terrorist person who attacks and scares other people

thatched roof covering of straw or reeds

unconscious knocked out, not awake

valour bravery

war crime crime committed during a war, such as killing people or treating prisoners very badly

Want to Know More?

Books

* *Christopher Reeve*, Philip Abraham (Children's Press, 2002)

* *Hero Dogs: Courageous Canines in Action*, Donna M. Jackson (Little, Brown, 2003)

* *The Great Serum Race: Blazing the Iditarod Trail*, Debbie S. Miller (Walker and Co., 2002)

Websites

* www.freethechildren.org
  Read about Free The Children. You could become a volunteer.

* www.myhero.com
  Find out about heroes, from animals to scientists. Talk about your own heroes.

* www.rolemodel.net
  Search through details of celebrities who have helped others.

If you liked this Atomic book, why don't you try these...?

Index

Notes for adults
Use the following questions to guide children towards identifying features of recount text:

Can you give an example of scene setting from page 6?
Can you find a recount of events on page 11?
Can you give examples of past tense language on page 15?
Can you find an example of a temporal connective on page 23?
Can you give an example of a closing statement from page 28?